Tangled Thoughts

Shelby McCormick

Copyright © 2023 Shelby McCormick

All rights reserved.

ISBN: 979-8-9887489-0-8

Contents

The Search	5
Surrender	6
Testimony	7
Shaken	8
Overcast	9
Thorns	10
Labels	11
Masquerade	12
Silhouettes	13
Missing Pieces	15
Scar Tissue	17
Darkness	22
Life's Vapor	24
Acid	25
Silent Voices	27
Tattered	30
Trials	31
Faded	32
Longing	34
Shadowy Outlines	35

*To all those who helped nurture my seed.
Thank you from the depths of my heart.*

The Search

Day in and day out,
we suffer from want.
This life never promises anything.
Yet, we demand
what we think we deserve.

We chase fame, fortune, and familiarity.
All of which are vapors,
appearing as something eternal.

They are merely temporal.
They will burn up and wither,
like the grass
under the heated sun.

Our souls long for something more;
we cannot seem to fill the gaping hole.

There's a hope that some speak of,
so distant, it appears unreal.

If only we could grasp this hope
– the only *real* everlasting
and steadfast thing
to which we can hold –
the hope of Jesus.

Surrender

Crack open my heart –
grant me a new start.
I want to be wholly Yours
until death takes me to the eternal shore.

I have lived my life only for myself
never caring for anyone else
but reality has set in
I now understand the weight of my sin.

I come before You
dirty and needing to be cleansed,
pleading You'd forgive me of my sins.

Testimony

I was lost, *now* I'm found.
I was bound, *now* I'm loosed.
Thank you, Jesus, for the cross.

Your mercy endureth forever,
slow to anger, quick to listen.
You hear my prayer when I draw nigh.

O Adonai, thank You for Your love.
Your sacrifice has set me free.
All that anguish You suffer'd for me.

I am loved by the only One who matters.
Thank You, Jesus, for never leaving.

It has been a long road,
but You've pulled me through.
Help me stay faithful –
no matter the cost.

Keep me steady, O Faithful and True!

shaken

Inspired by Psalm 40:2

the ground shakes beneath me
my strength fails to sustain me
as defeat overwhelms me

starting to sink in the sand beneath
a Rock rises
before me – strong and thick –

unwavering in strength
inviting me to grab hold
reaching out

my hand lays hold of it
holding me afloat
as the sand tries to suck me
down to the grave

left not in my own strength
but fully dependent on the Rock
i succumb to humility

for i stand on nothing of my own
nothing i did kept me from sinking
into the miry clay that day

only the Rock kept me afloat
as I hung on

Overcast

Gray – such a sad color,
  painting a picture of sadness and pain.

The clouds are gathering
  black and blue from the grief they hold.

Just beyond those eyes of yours
  are bodies of water begging to be released.

Just wait a little longer,
  until you can comfort yourself
in your sleep amidst your pool of dreams,
  where you may sip your tears for solace,
in dreaded fear of those nightmares.

Tears heal the unspoken brokenness.

Let the rain fall down your face;
  relieve your weary, burdened soul.
He sees you.
  Your promise *is* coming.

Thorns

Roses are red
or are they white?
Some used for the dead,
others for life.
Their green leaves speak
of a magnificent peak.

Oh, but roses have thorns
and life has thistles.

Labels

Mistaken... Dirty... Horrible...
Stupid... Worthless... Unloved...
Forgotten... Unforgivable... Unacceptable

Ever felt unaccepted?
Has your value been dragged through the dirt?
Have you been forgotten
or has some mistake
made you feel defeated?
It is a horrible place to be,
feeling past forgiveness.
Rejection leaves you feeling dirty,
But
the black denial of our failings
pales in comparison
to the golden reality of Jesus' scarlet blood.
God places intrinsic value
that we must view and own as truth.
We can choose all the fillers
but they will not fill the longing
for complete wholeness.
They will leave an aftertaste:
bitter and unsatisfying.

Masquerade

Shame is a shadow that haunts me,
  following me like a heavy chain.

Letting go is freedom,
  but the process is frightening.

This mask I wear gets heavy.
  My tears soil through.

Time to come out of the cage
  I have built around myself.

I seek You.

Silhouettes

The shadow of truth
A silhouette of life
a light burns in the distance
casting shadows of buried hopes on the ground.

Dark days are here;
they have chased the light away.

Graveyards of dreams and desires are scattered,
leaving a grim picture across my soul.

Silhouettes of things I once knew,
things now shrouded in illusion and mystery.

The lights have all gone out in my mind.
All but one little candle…
I hid it under a bushel,
too scared
the cruel gusts of this world would catch it.

Suddenly, the light faded out!

Suffocating the flame,
the bushel harms the light.

Lifting it, the candle roars up once more.
Shedding light across the rooms of my soul.

Color is brought back
into my Black and White life.

I can see the candle flame
growing in the gentle breeze

Missing Pieces

The feeling of missing pieces haunts me.
I reminisce the times I smiled more,
laughed a little harder,
enjoying life with no fear in sight.

A time where I had an amazing support group,
a lifeline in the midst of the storm.

A wonderful memory escapes my mind.
The ones I miss dearly
have long been shrouded in depressive darkness.

Overwhelming my mind,
you are the darkness
 – masquerading *yourself* as the
fear, shame, and guilt.

I opened the door,
but *you* locked it behind *you*.
All that was good in the world
has been shut out.

The windows have been barred.
The power cut off
from the outside.

I am an abandoned house –
empty and void of joy or company.
One day, a knock on the door reaches my ears.

Those demons which haunt me
sleep soundly.
Reaching for the knob I peek through.

A Man stands there.
Cracking the door open,
I stammer excuses for my dilapidated existence.
Only He nods while the door swings wider.

Stepping back, in shock, I watch
as this Outsider comes peacefully into my home.
He drives away those dark voices

and cleans the rooms I unlock for Him.
Praise the Lord!
He saw my abandoned house.

He was the piece to my puzzle.
My house, once a stranger to Love,
now knows His name.

Scar Tissue

Beat up by this world,
left like a dirty rag on the floor.
Stained by mistakes,
ignored by those you care for the most.

I have seen war.
The good and the bad playing
with the strings of my heart.
They pull hard against each other,
leaving me in heaped ruins.

When will my deliverance come?
I cannot trust in myself.
When will someone save me?

I hear a small voice say, "Come to me."
Yet, it feels so distant.
Almost out of reach and extremely quiet.

Like a ship lost at sea,
I am tossed in this ocean of emotion.
Where is stable ground?
Will I run ashore
or crash into the rocks of anxiety?

Precious Lord, lead me on.
May Your voice calm
the waters of this trial.
I hold fast to my Anchor.

The currents leave me dizzy;
my head spins in confusion.
Where do I turn for solace?
For peace?

The waves are crashing overboard.
The salt water penetrates my wounds,
stinging them and putrefying my dead flesh.

My struggles are like rope.
I become a victim as they surround my waist,
holding me down under their suppressive weight,
leaving a rash that burns.

How may I release these chains?
My sails are ripped.
My mending job was trash.

The stars are hiding from me.
I don't know where I am or where to go.
Navigation is all but lost. I am adrift at sea,
unseen except by the sharks who chase me.

Rescue is far over the horizon.
I am forgotten in the tempest of my trials.
Mankind has forgotten me and the heavens are
silent.

How much longer Lord?
How long will the storms last?
I cling to You, for You only can save.
Yet, why do You feel so far away?

Have I left Your side?
When? How?
Hear my cries for help, Oh Jesus!

Sleep comes in batches – sparingly.
Fitfully I toss in my sleep.
Dreams of hopes I cannot grasp
pass before my mind's eye.

Thoughts of future hopes and dreams
fade away as reality awakes me.
Sleep taunts me,

reminding me of my fears.
The fear of losing those I love and care for.
My ship is cracking from the weight of grief,

the cruel words of the world crashing against its sides.
A light flickers in the distance:
a search light in the storm.

Strength has left me.
Weakness takes over me like a virus,
corrupting me from inside out.

The search light passes over me;
I faint in despair.

As I succumb to the darkness,
a warm sensation passes over my salty,
dehydrated body.
Somewhere, someone lifts me up;

I swing helplessly in mid-air.
Is this what death feels like?
I have given up all expectations of being rescued.

I am put down.
My wounds feel the pain of medicine;
laughter heals my broken heart.
Why is it joyous

when I just left the wreckage of the storm…
dangling in the last hope?
Water is pressed to my lips and my heavy eyelids open.

A kind gentle face looks me in the eye.
He says, "O ye of little faith…
you have overcome the world in Me. You are Mine."

Exhausted, I collapse in His arms.
I awake healed in His kind embrace.
Slowly He passes me to another survivor.

They hold me up and support my shattered life.
The kind One that rescued me is replaced
by an equally sincere heart of compassion.

I am placed in the care of another.
I have found solace in this heart.
I have been placed under their care,
one who loves just as deeply,
and always will
until The Rescuer returns for the both of us.

The rain still terrifies me,
but now there is someone
who will stand by me
as the winds howl through my bones.

I am cared for.
The shipwreck was worth it,
for now I am stronger.
Let my heart show my gratitude
to the one who cared.

Darkness

It is cold but comforting.
  It tears at you,
and puts you back together.

The haunting moon gives light to those who
  daydream under its enchanted beams.
The stars guide the lost voyagers safely home.

Darkness, a deep void – a rebellious outcast
object.

Light purges and illuminates,
  revealing the deep, dark, hidden things.
Casting shadows that play with the mind,

foretelling of a substance
  – an obstacle in your path.
Remove it and you may lose comfort,

enduring shame only temporarily.
  O, the ecstasy of a clean, pure surface is
extraordinary!
That is, if you don't enjoy your dark company
  or your hiding places.

I find them comforting...
For He meets me there

When demons taunt you,
  know that angels surround you.
When you are surrounded,
  know that God sees you.

Wait and see the Lord of Hosts fight your battles!
  The dark may encompass you,
but take courage and be comforted,
  release your graveclothes of sin and shame.

Life's Vapor

Life is a vapor in time.
It fades and disappears,
like a shadow waiting to be grasped.

It propagates a false hope
of reliance on past things.
We look for healing in temporal bodies,

yet are not satisfied with what we find.
All of us are broken –
some more than others.

Not one person has a unique struggle.
The challenge is being *real*.
Society tries to force a mask on us,
fitting us into their mold.

BUT GOD

Calls us to be who He created us to be:

UNIQUE.

His Kingdom calls us to live this life worthy,
not to trash it for something
appearing good or desirable.

Acid

Sin creeps in like battery acid.
It corrodes and rusts away
our desire for godliness.
Overpowering our will,

turning the free will that is God-given
into that of a robotic mind: programmed.
Sin overrides our lives,

taking us in its desired destructive direction.
Slowly rusting our will-power and heart
into hardened,
unfeeling shards of metal.

The call of the Christian soldier:
to grab these wayward shackled souls
and bring them
to the knowledge of Christ and His Love.

Only His power can change
the work of the corrosive acid
– the delusion of sin corrupts our minds,
spreading like a fog,
clouding the intellect and conscience,
leading the imagination to dark visions,
forgetting the touch of fresh air,

captivated by the thought,
evermore enticing and entrapping:
this defective mirror of reality.

The true breath and enjoyment of life is lost
and remembered no more.
Those who notice reach out,
reminding the lost of the forbidden beauty
– the forgotten world in their dwindling memory.

The true beauty of life
found in the Joy coming from God only.
Never the incessant, varying, unreliable
happiness found in circumstances.

We follow a RISEN KING whose pathway is
belief and faith.
Trekking this narrow stairway
upstream through the busy current of the world.

Step too far out and you will get ripped away.
Without the TRUTH we become like
mesmerized fish;
bewildered sheep;
headlight-blinded deer;
lost puppies in need of a caring touch.

Easily set off track
but always
lovingly returned and accepted.

Silent Voices

Unheard, I cry.
Unseen, I weep.
Forgotten, I am left alone to mourn.

If a tree falls in the forest,
   does it make a sound?
If a heart breaks in a crowd,
  do we hear it shatter?

No.

The plight of the broken is a silent battle.
Defeated and worn down,
the warrior fights against things unseen.

Things he feels to a tremendous degree
– a warrior who forgets their worth.
Shattered hearts produce hearts callous to love.

They heal alone and forget what trust feels like.
Walked over like a doormat,
they close their hearts for visitation.

Only the patient knockers are allowed
inside their barricaded house of a soul.
These hearts are lights flickering in our dark world.

Their bright gleam is stolen away;
their existence is threatened
in the harsh cold wind of cruel words.

Their soft innocence
turned into a cold, hard light.
Where have lovingkindness and compassion
gone?

The world has lost its way.
Led by a fake moon, her course is set for wreckage
– an ill wind wishing her destruction.

Where is the shipmaster?
Who will grab the wheel?
Who will be the lookout?

Broken hearts fall like stars onto the deck.
They do not remember the true feeling of love and compassion.
Their hearts are thirst-stricken!

Parched by grief and abuse,
their throats constrict under pressure.
Their embrace is cold and absent.

They have forgotten the feeling of another's presence.
They are ignored, tattered, misused by others
who have forgotten the true essence of love.

These souls starve for forgiveness,
for healing and love beyond compare.
It is impossible to heal yourself,

even more so to make something of two broken
people.
Do not forget the power of love.
When true, it knows no boundary or distance.
One that forgives heartache and makes room for
growth.

Hold on, when the tears fall
and sorrow crashes aboard deck.
Hang on, when the world is tossed by the sea.

Don't forget your anchor.
Hold tightly to those you love
before they are tossed over in the night

by the water for the neglect
or dehydration
from the taste of care.

Tattered

Tattered are the wings which once flew
Shattered by bullets of expectancy
They have forgotten the feeling of air
underneath.

Soaring no more into the clouds of hope,
they plunge to the depths of despair.
The dark abyss welcomes the worn-down
creature with gaping jaws.

Before it closes forever shut,
a gust of wind lifts the delicate wings,
bringing them to land on soft cherished hopes.

A soft refreshing dew bathes the wings
that were once stretched thin.
Breathing life into the weathered and torn lace,

the sunshine warms the creature and refreshes it
anew.
So too have my hopes been demolished,
battered down by the storms of life

only to be taken up by God
and breathed in once more.

Trials

Growth is painful.
  The lengthening of patience is trying.
Sometimes, in the hard moments,

we forget to breathe.
  We hold in our pain,
keeping back the waters

which threaten to spill down our face.
  Often, the only way to heal
is to express it.

The hardest part —
  is letting go of the pain.
Especially when we have become so used to it…

We become scared of freedom
– like a bird,
whose cage door has opened,
  is afraid to leave.

Faded

A fog has come to rest on my mind.
Every memory I once cherished
has become dreary and dim

Forgetting faces and names
I remember the feelings only
Even the sound of their voices grows mute

I wish to renew those memories afresh
And drive the fog away
I do not mind clouds,

for there are some things
  which need to be blocked for a time

Only never forget me,
for I oft think of you

✻ ✻ ✻

Has your memory plagued you
with lies and deception?
Has the cool front of harsh words
driven in the mists of loneliness?

Do not forsake those who shine hope in your life.

Even when you find comfort
in your starlit walks of the inner soul.
Never lose sight of the moon

for she always radiates light from her sun.
He is the one to whom
she knows where he will forever be

Only let her rest from time to time
and find a new phase.
For sometimes that sun whom she radiates
is not the true one.

Let her radiate the bright
and shining Son whose light will never fade.

The world brings darkness and fades
the light exposing the false suns.

Focus on the true one
and let Him be your guiding source
of warmth and compassion.

Longing

Casting a line and reeling in nothing
  The current rips at the line
tugging your expectations.

Only to leave you with an empty hook
 A clean ripoff – like Velcro
The more you use it the less it stays.

The harder you try to fix someone
  who just wants to grab and take,
the more tattered you will become.

Shadowy outlines

They are all I see in this world.
Masquerading guilt and shame,
we wear our masks to the dance of life.

Deceiving humanity
with fancy lies and half truths.

Who is brave enough to come without a mask?
Who wants to show their naked soul?

We memorize the right things.
We keep in time with the rhythm.
Making sure no one sees us when we miscount
the steps.

Dance the right moves.
Wear your best.
Deceive the world so you may avoid its insults.

But oh darling, show your true heart.
'Til your cracks and your flaws
show your strength, the battles you have
overcome.

Dance without a partner if you must!
Wait til one steps in willing to take off their
facade.

And dance into the night with them.
Stay with them through the morning.

For they will stay with you in the rain.
They will not run for cover when the clouds roll through.

Until then, dance with sincerity.
Be raw and prepare for another brave soul.

Your facade is wearing off.
I want to see who is behind that feathered mask.
Show me your raw beauty. Your aching soul.
Show me where to love you and make you whole.

There are too many fake people in this world.
Be true to you and show yourself.
Show who you are.

It takes courage.
Undying courage.

The world is full of spineless followers.
She needs brave people who wish to break the mold.
To break the yoke of societal reforms and social graces.

Become free!
Do not succumb to the rules of the ball,
this dance we call life.

For when the clock strikes midnight and the owner comes,
The spell of deception will cease.
The masks will come off.

Make sure you dance
with someone you know and not a monster
covered by a rose-colored mask.

Charm is deceptive.
Pride is a downfall.
Learn from your mistakes when you dance.
Don't be afraid to fall behind and start again.

Always dance hard and true,
Live and love unashamedly.

Until next time…

www.ingramcontent.com/pod-product-compliance
Lightning Source LLC
Chambersburg PA
CBHW061348040426
42444CB00011B/3141